Elevate Your Knitting Skills with Textures

Essential Techniques in this Book

Dixia I Nolan

THIS BOOK BELONGS TO

The Library of

....

....

Thank you for Purchasing my book and taking the time to read it from front to back. I am always grateful when a reader chooses my work and I hope you enjoyed it!

With the vast selection available online, I am touched that you chose to be purchasing my work and take valuable time out of your life to read it. My hope is that you feel you made the right decision.

I very much would like to know what you thought of the book. Please take the time to write an honest and informative review on Amazon.com. Your experience and opinions will be of great benefit to me and those readers looking to make an informed choice.

With much thanks.

Table of Contents

SUMMARY

The Magic of Simple Stitches: How Knit and Purl Shape Knitting:

Knitting is a craft that has been practiced for centuries, and its popularity continues to grow. From cozy sweaters to intricate lace shawls, the possibilities are endless when it comes to creating beautiful and functional pieces with just a few simple stitches. One of the most fundamental stitches in knitting is the knit stitch, also known as the plain stitch. This stitch creates a smooth and flat fabric, perfect for garments and accessories. On the other hand, the purl stitch adds texture and depth to the fabric, making it ideal for creating patterns and designs.

The beauty of knitting lies in the combination of these two basic stitches, knit and purl. By alternating between them, you can create a wide range of stitch patterns that can shape your knitting in various ways. The way you arrange these stitches can determine the overall look and feel of your project, whether it's a cozy scarf or a delicate baby blanket.

When you knit every stitch in a row, you create what is called the garter stitch. This stitch pattern is reversible, meaning it looks the same on both sides, making it a versatile choice for scarves and blankets. The garter stitch also has a natural elasticity, making it a great option for projects that require stretch, such as hats or socks.

On the other hand, when you alternate between knitting and purling in a row, you create what is known as the stockinette stitch. This stitch pattern creates a smooth and flat fabric on one side, with rows of "V" shapes formed by the knit stitches. The other side of the fabric has rows of purl bumps. The stockinette stitch is commonly used for garments, as it creates a polished and professional look. However, it is important to note that the stockinette stitch tends to curl at the edges, so it is often paired with a border or finished with ribbing to prevent this.

By combining knit and purl stitches in different patterns, you can create a variety of textures and designs. For example, the seed stitch is created by alternating between knit and purl stitches in a row, and then switching the pattern in the next row. This stitch pattern creates a bumpy texture that resembles scattered seeds, hence its name. The moss stitch, on the other hand, is created by alternating between knit and purl stitches for two rows, and then switching the pattern for the next two rows.

The Infinite Possibilities of Texture in Knitting: Knitting, a craft that has been practiced for centuries, offers an infinite array of possibilities when it comes to texture. From simple garter stitch to intricate cable patterns, the texture in knitting can add depth, interest, and even functionality to a finished piece.

One of the simplest ways to create texture in knitting is through the use of different stitch patterns. Garter stitch, for example, is created by knitting every row, resulting in a bumpy, textured fabric. On the other hand, stockinette stitch, which is created by knitting one row and purling the next, creates a smooth, flat fabric. By combining these basic stitches, knitters can create a wide variety of textures, from ribbing to seed stitch to basketweave.

Beyond basic stitch patterns, knitters can also incorporate more complex techniques to create texture. Cables, for example, are created by crossing stitches over each other, resulting in a raised, three-dimensional pattern. This technique can be used to create intricate designs, such as braids or twists, that add visual interest and depth to a knitted piece. Lace knitting, on the other hand, involves creating deliberate holes in the fabric by increasing and decreasing stitches. This technique can create delicate, airy textures that are perfect for lightweight garments or accessories.

Texture in knitting can also serve a functional purpose. For example, by using a combination of knit and purl stitches, knitters can create a fabric that is more elastic and stretchy, making it ideal for garments that need to fit snugly, such as socks or hats. Additionally, certain stitch patterns, such as the brioche stitch, create a reversible fabric with a unique texture on both sides. This can be particularly useful for items like scarves or blankets, where both sides of the fabric will be visible.

The possibilities for texture in knitting are truly endless. By experimenting with different stitch patterns, techniques, and yarns, knitters can create pieces that are not only visually stunning but also have a tactile quality that is a joy to touch and wear. Whether it's a cozy sweater with intricate cables, a delicate lace shawl, or a chunky blanket with a bumpy texture, the art of knitting allows for endless exploration and creativity when it comes to texture.

Navigating the Landscape of This Guide in Knitting: When it comes to knitting, there is a vast landscape of techniques, patterns, and resources to explore. This guide aims to help you navigate this landscape and make the most of your knitting journey.

First and foremost, it is important to understand the basics of knitting. This includes learning about different types of yarn, understanding knitting needles and their sizes, and familiarizing yourself with common knitting terms and abbreviations. This guide will provide you with a comprehensive overview of these foundational aspects, ensuring that you have a solid understanding before diving into more advanced techniques.

Once you have a good grasp of the basics, you can start exploring different knitting techniques. From simple stitches like the knit and purl to more complex techniques like cables and lace, there is a wide range of techniques to learn and master. This guide will walk you through each technique step-by-step, providing clear instructions and helpful tips along the way. Whether you are a beginner or an experienced knitter looking to expand your skillset, this guide has something for everyone.

In addition to techniques, this guide also covers various knitting patterns. From basic scarves and hats to intricate sweaters and shawls, there are countless patterns available for knitters of all levels. This guide will introduce you to different types of patterns, explain how to read and interpret them, and provide recommendations for finding patterns that suit your style and skill level. With the help of this guide, you will be able to confidently tackle any knitting project you set your sights on.

Furthermore, this guide recognizes the importance of resources in the knitting community. Whether it's books, online tutorials, or knitting groups, there are numerous resources available to support and inspire knitters. This guide will highlight some of the best resources out there, helping you connect with fellow knitters, find inspiration, and expand your knowledge. Additionally, it will provide guidance on how to troubleshoot common knitting problems and offer suggestions for organizing your knitting supplies and projects.

Overall, this guide is designed to be a comprehensive and user-friendly resource for anyone interested in knitting. Whether you are a beginner looking to get started or an experienced knitter seeking new challenges, this guide will provide you with the knowledge and tools you need to navigate the vast landscape of knitting. So grab your needles and yarn, and let's embark on this knitting journey together.

The Fundamental Stitches: Knit Stitch: The knit stitch is one of the fundamental stitches in knitting. It is a versatile stitch that is commonly used in various knitting projects. The knit stitch creates a smooth and flat fabric with a "V" shape pattern on the right side and a series of horizontal bumps on the wrong side.

To execute the knit stitch, you will need a pair of knitting needles and yarn. Start by holding the knitting needle with the cast-on stitches in your left hand. Insert the right needle into the first stitch from left to right, going under the left needle. The right needle should be behind the left needle.

Next, bring the yarn over the right needle from back to front, creating a loop around the right needle. This loop is called a "yarn over." With the yarn over in place, use the right needle to pull it through the first stitch on the left needle, creating a new stitch on the right needle.

Once the new stitch is on the right needle, slide the original stitch off the left needle, allowing it to rest on the right needle. Repeat these steps for each stitch on the left needle until all the stitches have been transferred to the right needle.

The knit stitch can be worked in different ways, depending on the desired outcome. The most common method is called the English or throwing method, where the yarn is held in the right hand and thrown over the right needle to create the yarn over. Another method is the

Continental or picking method, where the yarn is held in the left hand and picked with the right needle to create the yarn over. Both methods produce the same result, so choose the one that feels most comfortable for you.

The knit stitch is often used as the foundation for many knitting patterns. It can be used to create a variety of textures and patterns, such as stockinette stitch, garter stitch, ribbing, and cables. By combining knit stitches with other stitches, you can create intricate designs and beautiful garments.

In addition to its versatility, the knit stitch is also relatively easy to learn and master. With practice, you can develop a smooth and consistent tension, resulting in even and professional-looking stitches. It is important to maintain an even tension throughout your knitting to ensure that your finished project has a uniform appearance.

Overall, the knit stitch is an essential skill for any knitter. Whether you are a beginner or an experienced knitter, mastering the knit stitch opens up a world of possibilities for creating beautiful and unique knitted items.

The Fundamental Stitches: Purl Stitch: The purl stitch is one of the fundamental stitches in knitting. It is commonly used to create a smooth and textured fabric, and is often paired with the knit stitch to create various patterns and designs.

To execute the purl stitch, you will need a pair of knitting needles and a ball of yarn. Begin by holding the knitting needle with the cast-on stitches in your left hand, and the empty needle in your right hand. Insert the right needle into the first stitch on the left needle, from right to left, as if you were going to knit.

Next, take the yarn and bring it to the front of your work, between the two needles. With your right hand, wrap the yarn around the right needle, moving it from back to front. The yarn should now be positioned in front of the right needle.

Now, take the right needle and bring it towards you, through the stitch on the left needle. The right needle should be inserted from right to left, going under the left needle. This will create a loop of yarn around the right needle.

With the loop of yarn on the right needle, use your right hand to pull the right needle and the loop of yarn through the stitch on the left needle. This will transfer the stitch from the left needle to the right needle, and create a new stitch on the right needle.

Once you have completed the purl stitch, you can slide the original stitch off the left needle, leaving the new stitch on the right needle. Repeat these steps for each stitch on the left needle until you have completed the row.

The purl stitch creates a series of bumps on the right side of the fabric, and a smooth surface on the wrong side. It is often used to create ribbing, which is a stretchy and elastic fabric commonly found on cuffs, collars, and hems.

By combining the purl stitch with the knit stitch, you can create a wide variety of patterns and textures in your knitting. Experiment with different combinations and stitch counts to create unique and personalized designs.

Remember to practice and be patient when learning the purl stitch. It may take some time to get the tension and rhythm right, but with practice, you will be able to execute the stitch smoothly and confidently.

The Interplay of Knit and Purl Stitches: The interplay of knit and purl stitches is a fundamental aspect of knitting that allows for the creation of a wide range of textures and patterns. Knitting involves working with two basic stitches: the knit stitch and the purl stitch. These two stitches are the building blocks of all knitting projects and can be combined in various ways to achieve different effects.

The knit stitch is created by inserting the right-hand needle into the front of the stitch on the left-hand needle, wrapping the yarn around the right-hand needle, and pulling it through the stitch. This creates a new stitch on the right-hand needle while the old stitch is transferred from the left-hand needle. The purl stitch, on the other hand, is created by inserting the right-hand needle into the front of the stitch on the left-hand needle, but instead of wrapping the yarn around the needle, the yarn is brought to the front of the work. The right-hand needle is then inserted into the back of the stitch, and the yarn is pulled through to create a new stitch.

The interplay of knit and purl stitches allows for the creation of various stitch patterns, such as ribbing, seed stitch, and moss stitch. Ribbing is a common stitch pattern used for cuffs, collars, and hems, and it is created by alternating knit and purl stitches in a specific sequence. This creates a stretchy and elastic fabric that is often used for garments that need to fit closely to the body. Seed stitch, on the other hand, is created by alternating knit and purl stitches in a random sequence. This creates a textured fabric with small bumps that resemble seeds. Moss stitch is similar to seed stitch but is created by working a knit stitch into a purl stitch and a purl stitch into a knit stitch. This creates a fabric with a more pronounced texture.

The interplay of knit and purl stitches also allows for the creation of more complex stitch patterns, such as cables and lace. Cables are created by crossing stitches over each other, which is achieved by working certain stitches out of order. This creates a twisted effect that resembles a cable. Lace patterns, on the other hand, are created by strategically increasing and decreasing stitches to create holes and intricate designs. These patterns often require a combination of knit and purl stitches to achieve the desired effect.

In conclusion, the interplay of knit and purl stitches is a fundamental aspect of knitting that allows for the creation of a wide range of textures and patterns.

Understanding 1x1, 2x2, and Varied Ribbing Patterns in Knitting: Knitting is a popular craft that involves creating fabric by interlocking loops of yarn with knitting needles. One of the fundamental techniques in knitting is understanding and using different ribbing patterns. Ribbing is a type of stitch pattern that creates a stretchy and elastic fabric, commonly used for cuffs, collars, and hems in garments.

There are several types of ribbing patterns, including 1x1 and 2x2 ribbing. The numbers in these patterns refer to the number of knit stitches and purl stitches in each repeat. In 1x1 ribbing, one knit stitch is followed by one purl stitch, creating a simple alternating pattern. This pattern is often used for cuffs and edges, as it provides a neat and flexible finish. On the other hand, 2x2 ribbing consists of two knit stitches followed by two purl stitches, creating a more pronounced ribbed effect. This pattern is commonly used for sweaters and scarves, as it provides a more textured and visually interesting fabric.

To create these ribbing patterns, you will need to have a basic understanding of knitting stitches. Knit stitches are created by inserting the needle into the front of the stitch on the left needle, wrapping the yarn around the right needle, and pulling it through the stitch. Purl stitches, on the other hand, are created by inserting the needle into the front of the stitch on the left needle, but wrapping the yarn around the right needle in the opposite direction. This creates a twisted loop, resulting in a different texture.

When working with ribbing patterns, it is important to maintain tension and consistency in your stitches. This ensures that the ribbing is even and the fabric has the desired stretchiness. It is also important to pay attention to the pattern instructions, as they will specify the number of stitches and rows needed to create the desired ribbing effect.

In addition to 1x1 and 2x2 ribbing, there are also varied ribbing patterns that incorporate different combinations of knit and purl stitches. These patterns can create more intricate and unique textures in the fabric. For example, a 3x1 ribbing pattern consists of three knit stitches followed by one purl stitch, creating a wider ribbed effect. This pattern can be used to add visual interest to a garment or accessory.

Overall, understanding and using different ribbing patterns in knitting allows you to create fabric with different textures and stretchiness.

Projects Ideal for Basketweave and Checkered Textures in Knitting: When it comes to knitting projects, there are a variety of textures that can be incorporated to add visual interest and depth to your creations. Two popular textures that are often used in knitting are basketweave and checkered patterns. These patterns not only provide a unique look to your projects but also offer a great opportunity to showcase your knitting skills.

The basketweave texture is characterized by its interlocking squares, resembling the pattern of a woven basket. This texture is achieved by alternating blocks of knit and purl stitches, creating a visually appealing design. Basketweave patterns are versatile and can be used in a wide range of knitting projects, from scarves and hats to blankets and sweaters. The texture adds a touch of sophistication and elegance to any item, making it a great choice for more formal or dressy pieces.

On the other hand, checkered patterns are created by alternating blocks of two different colors, typically in a square or rectangular shape. This texture is achieved by using a combination of knit and purl stitches, creating a checkerboard-like design. Checkered patterns are perfect for adding a playful and fun element to your knitting projects. They can be used in various items such as baby blankets, dishcloths, and even socks. The contrasting colors in the checkered pattern make it visually appealing and eye-catching.

When choosing knitting projects that are ideal for basketweave and checkered textures, it is important to consider the size and complexity of the pattern. Basketweave patterns tend to be more intricate and require a bit more attention to detail, making them better suited for larger projects such as blankets or sweaters. On the other hand, checkered patterns can be easily incorporated into smaller projects like scarves or hats, as they are relatively simpler to execute.

Additionally, the type of yarn you choose can also impact the overall look and feel of the basketweave or checkered texture. For basketweave patterns, using a yarn with good stitch definition, such as a smooth worsted weight yarn, will help showcase the intricate details of the pattern. For checkered patterns, using yarns with contrasting colors will enhance the visual impact of the design.

In conclusion, basketweave and checkered textures are popular choices in knitting projects due to their versatility and visual appeal. Whether you're looking to create a sophisticated and elegant piece or a playful and fun item, incorporating these textures into your knitting projects can add depth and interest.

Exploring the Double Seed Stitch in Knitting: The Double Seed Stitch is a versatile and visually appealing knitting stitch pattern that adds texture and depth to any project. It is a variation of the Seed Stitch, which is known for its alternating knit and purl stitches. The Double Seed Stitch takes this pattern to the next level by repeating the sequence of knit and purl stitches twice, creating a more pronounced texture.

To create the Double Seed Stitch, you will need a pair of knitting needles and a ball of yarn in your desired color. Start by casting on an even number of stitches. The Double Seed Stitch works best with a multiple of four stitches, but you can adjust the number to fit your project.

Once you have cast on your stitches, the pattern begins with two rows of knit stitches. This creates a solid base for the seed stitch pattern. After the initial knit rows, you will start the sequence of knit and purl stitches.

The first row of the pattern is as follows: *K2, P2*. Repeat this sequence until the end of the row. The second row is the reverse: *P2, K2*. Repeat this sequence until the end of the row. These two rows create the foundation of the Double Seed Stitch pattern.

To continue the pattern, simply repeat these two rows until you have reached your desired length. The Double Seed Stitch is reversible, meaning it looks the same on both sides, making it perfect for scarves, blankets, and other items where both sides will be visible.

The Double Seed Stitch is a great option for beginners as it only requires basic knitting skills. It is also a great stitch pattern for practicing tension and gauge, as the alternating knit and purl stitches create a tight and even fabric.

One of the advantages of the Double Seed Stitch is its versatility. It can be used in a variety of projects, from simple accessories to more complex garments. It adds texture and interest to plain stockinette stitch or can be combined with other stitch patterns for a unique look.

When working with the Double Seed Stitch, it is important to pay attention to your tension. The alternating knit and purl stitches can sometimes cause the fabric to become tighter or looser than desired. Make sure to keep your tension consistent throughout your project to achieve a uniform appearance.

In conclusion, the Double Seed Stitch is a beautiful and versatile knitting stitch pattern that adds texture and depth to any project. Whether you are a beginner or an experienced knitter, this stitch is a great option for creating visually appealing and unique pieces.

Crafting Diagonal Ribs and Textures in Knitting: Crafting diagonal ribs and textures in knitting is a technique that adds depth and visual interest to your knitted projects. By incorporating diagonal lines and textured stitches, you can create unique and eye-catching patterns that elevate your knitting skills to the next level.

To begin crafting diagonal ribs, you will need to have a basic understanding of knitting techniques such as knit and purl stitches. Diagonal ribs are created by working increases and decreases in a specific pattern, which results in a slanted design. This technique can be used to create a variety of patterns, from simple diagonal lines to more intricate designs.

One popular method for creating diagonal ribs is the "knit one below" technique. This involves knitting into the stitch below the next stitch on your left-hand needle, which creates a slanted stitch. By repeating this technique across a row, you can create a diagonal rib pattern that adds a dynamic element to your knitting.

Another way to incorporate diagonal ribs is by using twisted stitches. Twisted stitches are created by knitting or purling through the back loop of a stitch, which twists the stitch and creates a diagonal line. By combining twisted stitches with regular knit and purl stitches, you can create a textured fabric with diagonal ribs.

In addition to diagonal ribs, you can also experiment with different textures in your knitting. Textured stitches, such as cables, bobbles, and seed stitch, can add depth and dimension to your projects. These stitches create raised or recessed areas in your knitting, which can be used to create patterns or motifs.

Cables are a popular textured stitch that can be used to create diagonal patterns. By crossing stitches over each other, you can create a cable that slants in a diagonal direction. This technique can be used to create intricate cable patterns or simple diagonal lines, depending on your preference.

Bobbles are another textured stitch that can be used to create interesting patterns. By working a series of increases and decreases in a small area, you can create a raised bump or bobble on your knitting. By strategically placing these bobbles in a diagonal pattern, you can create a unique and visually appealing design.

Seed stitch is a simple textured stitch that can be used to create a subtle diagonal pattern. By alternating knit and purl stitches in a specific pattern, you can create a fabric with a textured, pebbled appearance. This stitch is versatile and can be used in a variety of projects, from scarves to sweaters.

Chevron Patterns and Their Zigzag Beauty in Knitting: Chevron patterns are a popular choice among knitters due to their visually appealing zigzag design. These patterns create a sense of movement and add a dynamic element to any knitted project. Whether you're a beginner or an experienced knitter, incorporating chevron patterns into your work can elevate your knitting skills and create stunning finished pieces.

The beauty of chevron patterns lies in their versatility. They can be used in a variety of knitting projects, including scarves, blankets, sweaters, and even socks. The zigzag design adds a touch of sophistication and elegance to any item, making it a great choice for both casual and formal wear.

One of the reasons why chevron patterns are so popular is because they are relatively easy to knit. They typically involve simple increases and decreases, which are basic knitting techniques that most knitters are familiar with. This makes chevron patterns accessible to knitters of all skill levels, including beginners who are looking to expand their repertoire.

In addition to their simplicity, chevron patterns also offer endless possibilities for customization. Knitters can experiment with different color combinations to create unique and eye-catching designs. Whether you prefer bold and vibrant colors or subtle and muted tones, chevron patterns can be adapted to suit your personal style and preferences.

Furthermore, chevron patterns can be easily modified to create different effects. By adjusting the number of stitches or the size of the zigzag, you can create variations of the classic chevron design. This allows you to tailor the pattern to fit the specific dimensions of your project or to achieve a desired visual effect.

When knitting with chevron patterns, it's important to pay attention to tension and gauge. Maintaining an even tension throughout your work will ensure that the zigzag design remains crisp and well-defined. Additionally, checking your gauge before starting a project will help you determine the appropriate needle size and yarn weight to use, resulting in a finished piece that matches the intended measurements.

In conclusion, chevron patterns are a fantastic choice for knitters who want to add a touch of elegance and movement to their projects. With their versatility, simplicity, and endless customization options, chevron patterns offer a world of creative possibilities. So grab your knitting needles, choose your favorite colors, and start creating beautiful zigzag designs that will impress everyone who sees your work.

Designing with Diagonal and Chevron Textures in Knitting: Designing with Diagonal and Chevron Textures in Knitting is a comprehensive guide that explores the various techniques and patterns that can be used to create stunning and visually appealing designs in knitting. This book is a must-have for both beginner and experienced knitters who are looking to add a touch of sophistication and elegance to their projects.

The book begins by introducing the concept of diagonal and chevron textures in knitting and explains how these patterns can be achieved using different stitches and techniques. It provides step-by-step instructions and detailed illustrations to help readers understand and master these techniques.

One of the highlights of this book is the wide range of patterns and designs that are included. From simple and subtle diagonal textures to bold and intricate chevron patterns, there is something for everyone in this book. Each pattern is accompanied by clear and concise instructions, making it easy for knitters of all skill levels to follow along and create beautiful projects.

In addition to the patterns, the book also offers valuable tips and tricks for designing with diagonal and chevron textures. It discusses how to choose the right yarn and needles for each project, as well as how to modify and customize patterns to suit individual preferences. The book also provides guidance on color selection and how to create stunning color combinations that enhance the overall design.

Furthermore, Designing with Diagonal and Chevron Textures in Knitting goes beyond just providing patterns and instructions. It delves into the theory and principles behind these textures, explaining how they can be used to create different effects and moods in knitting. It also explores the history and cultural significance of these patterns, giving readers a deeper appreciation for the art of knitting.

Whether you are a seasoned knitter looking to expand your repertoire or a beginner eager to learn new techniques, Designing with Diagonal and Chevron Textures in Knitting is the ultimate resource for creating stunning and unique designs. With its comprehensive instructions, inspiring patterns, and insightful tips, this book is sure to become a cherished companion for any knitting enthusiast.

How to Cardigans that Showcase Knit and Purl Patterns in Knitting: If you're looking to create cardigans that beautifully showcase knit and purl patterns in knitting, you've come to the right place! Knitting cardigans with intricate knit and purl patterns can add a touch of elegance and sophistication to your wardrobe. Whether you're a beginner or an experienced knitter, this guide will provide you with the necessary steps and tips to create stunning cardigans that highlight these patterns.

First and foremost, it's important to choose the right yarn for your project. Opt for a yarn that has good stitch definition, meaning that the individual stitches are clearly visible. This will help to enhance the knit and purl patterns in your cardigan. Additionally, consider the weight and fiber content of the yarn. Thicker yarns will create a more pronounced texture, while lighter yarns will result in a more delicate and subtle pattern. Experiment with different yarns to find the perfect match for your desired cardigan design.

Once you have your yarn, it's time to select a suitable pattern. There are countless knitting patterns available that incorporate various knit and purl stitches. Look for patterns that specifically highlight these stitches or have sections where you can incorporate them. Some popular choices include cable patterns, lace patterns, and textured stitch patterns. These patterns often feature a combination of knit and purl stitches, allowing you to showcase your skills and create visually appealing cardigans.

Before diving into your project, it's essential to swatch. Swatching involves knitting a small sample of your chosen pattern to determine the correct gauge and ensure that your finished cardigan will fit properly. This step is often overlooked but is crucial for achieving the desired results. Take the time to knit a swatch using the same needles and yarn you plan to use for your cardigan. Measure the gauge and compare it to the pattern instructions. Adjust your needle size if necessary to achieve the correct gauge. Swatching will save you from potential disappointment and frustration later on.

Once you have your gauge and are confident in your chosen pattern, it's time to start knitting your cardigan. Follow the pattern instructions carefully, paying close attention to the knit and purl stitches. Take your time and enjoy the process of creating intricate patterns. If you're new to knitting, it may be helpful to practice the specific stitches before starting your cardigan. This will help you become more comfortable with the techniques and ensure that your stitches are even and consistent throughout your project.

Chapter One – Yarn and Needles

In this chapter we'll learn the basics of yarn and needles. This information is important to learn because you can then choose the correct yarn and needle type for every project.

Yarn

Yarn comes in three main types of fibers; animal, plant, and synthetic. Animal fibers include wool, alpaca, cashmere, angora, and silk. Plant fibers include cotton, hemp, soy, bamboo, and linen. Synthetic fibers include acrylic, polyester, microfiber, and metallic threads. Each type of yarn has its benefits. For example, wool yarn works up into a nice warm spongy fabric, while cotton yarn is stiffer and soaks up moisture. Acrylic yarn is suitable for many projects, and is a cost effective and easy to work with choice for beginners and more advanced knitting artists alike.

Blocking

Animal and plant fiber based yarn looks best if the projects are blocked once you have completed them. Blocking relaxes the yarn fibers and brings out the stitch definition. Blocking is also important for garments so you get the correct fit.

Once you have finished your project soak it in water and then roll it up in a big fluffy towel to remove the excess moisture. Do not ring the towel as this may damage the knitting. On either blocking mats or another big towel take some blocking or sewing pins and begin shaping the project. Pin the outer edges shaping the fabric as needed. You may need to move the pins as you block. Once you're happy with the shape of the fabric, let it dry completely before you take the pins out.

You can also use a spray bottle of water for smaller projects. Pin the fabric onto blocking mats or a big towel and then gently mist the fabric with water. Let dry completely and remove the pins.

While acrylic or synthetic yarn rarely needs to be blocked, you can block them with steam. Pin the fabric onto blocking mats or a big towel and then very carefully use a steam iron and apply steam gently to the fabric. Hold the iron up off the fabric and do not iron directly onto the knitting. You may need to readjust the pins once you steam the fabric. Let dry completely before you remove the pins.

Yarn Weight and Gauge

Yarn comes in several different weights from lace and fingerling to super bulky jumbo yarn. Each weight of yarn has a recommended needle size which will give you a specific gauge. Gauge refers to how many stitches it takes to create four inches of fabric across the rows, and how many rows it takes to create four inches of knit fabric.

It is a good practice to knit up a gauge swatch before you begin a pattern. Your tension may affect the gauge and you may need to go up or down a needle size to obtain the correct gauge. Knit up a swatch of material and count the stitches across a four-inch row. Now count the rows in four inches. This is the gauge.

In the following table you can see if you use a medium weight yarn with a size 7 to 9 needle you will have 16 to 20 stitches across a row of four inches. As the yarn weight increases or decreases, the gauge also increases or decreases.

This is why it is important to check the yarn and needle size for each pattern. If you use a yarn which is too light with small needles your project will be much smaller than you intended.

Yarn Weight Chart				
	Weight	**Description**	**Recommended Needle Size**	**Stitches in 4"**
0	Lace	Fingerling, Size 10 Crochet Thread	000-1/1.5-2.25mm	33-40
1	Superfine	Sock, Fingerling	1-3/2.25-3.25mm	27-32
2	Fine	Sport, Baby	3-5/3.25-3.75mm	23-26
3	Light	DK, Light Worsted	5-7/3.75-4.5mm	21-24
4	Medium	Worsted, Afghan, Aran	7-9/3.75-4.5mm	16-20

5	Bulky	Chunky, Craft, Rug	9-11/5.5-8mm	12-15
6	Super Bulky	Super Bulky, Roving	11-17/8-12.75mm	7-11
7	Jumbo	Jumbo, Roving	17/12.75mm and up	6 or less

How to Read a Yarn Label

When you go to purchase yarn, the information you need is all contained on the yarn label. The label will tell you the weight of the yarn, the gauge using the recommended needle size, and how to care for the finished project. It will also tell you what materials were used to create the yarn. Yarn manufacturers use a standardized set of laundry care symbols on their labels. You can find a complete list of these symbols at the Lion Brand site. I recommend printing the off and putting them near your washer and dryer for reference.

This yarn label is from a skein of Red Heart Super Saver Cherry Red yarn. As you can see, it is an acrylic yarn with a gauge of 17 stitches and 23 rows when using a size US 8 (5mm) needle. The weight class is 4, or medium. According to the laundry care symbols, this yarn can be machine washed and dried no hotter than 104F. The label also tells you the skein is center pull. Skeins pull from the center, while balls (which can also look like skiens) are pulled from the outside.

Knitting needles come in three main types: straight, circular, and double pointed. Straight needles are used for projects which are knitted back and forth in rows. Circular needles are used for knitting in the round, and to hold a large number of stitches in projects worked in rows. Double pointed needles allow you to knit small projects in the round such as hats and other project which would be too small to fit on a circular needle.

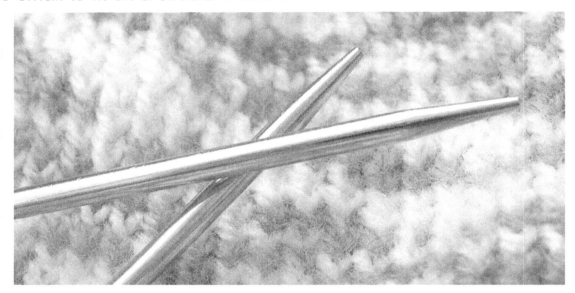

Straight Needles

Circular Needles

Double Pointed Needles

Other Equipment

Cable needles are curved needles used to hold stitches as you knit cables. Stitch holders look like huge safety pins and are used to hold a group of stitches while you knit. Row counters are handy to help you keep track of which row you are working on, and a flat or tapestry needle is also needed to weave in tails and sew pieces of knitting together. Markers are round circles which slip onto the needle to help you mark pattern repeats, the beginning of a round, and to guide you in a pattern. A good pair of scissors, or shears, is also an essential tool.

Chapter Two – Essential Knitting Stitches and Techniques

In this chapter we'll finally put some yarn on the needles and begin to knit. Remember if you're just starting out to take it slow. It will take a while to get used to handling the yarn and needles, so relax. You may have to rip out stitches, I still do. You may also drop some stitches, I still do that too. We'll learn how to pick up dropped stitches, and how to use a lifeline to help you if you have to rip out a section of your work. Concentrate on technique, not speed. Speed will come later with practice, for now enjoy yourself and relax!

Casting On

Before you actually knit any stitches you must first get the yarn onto the needles. This is known as casting on. In patterns you may see the abbreviation CO for cast on. In this section we'll learn some of my favorite and easy ways to cast on.

Backwards Loop Method

One of the easiest methods is the backwards loop method. Place a slip knot onto the needle. In your left hand hold the yarn with the yarn from the skein over your thumb and the tail over your index finger. With your right hand pull the yarn between your thumb and index finger down and insert the tip into the loop formed around your thumb. Release the yarn and wrap the yarn around the needle cast on the stitch. Repeat until you have the correct number of stitches cast on.

The advantage to the method is it is very quick and easy, but it makes a tight cast on row which can be hard to work with for beginners.

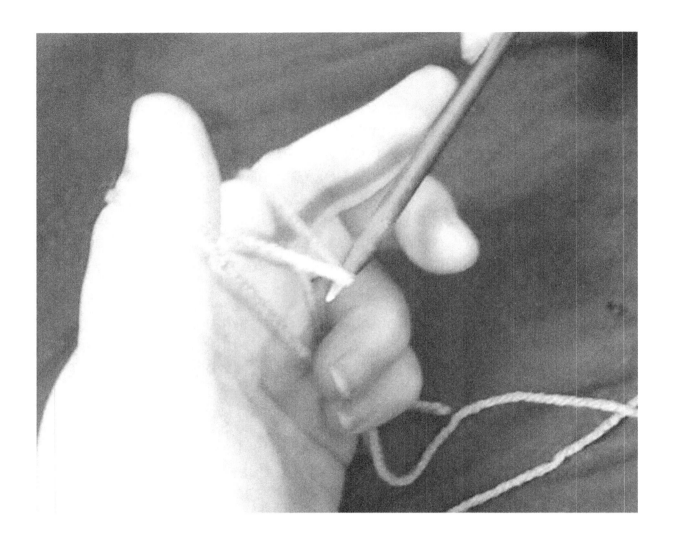

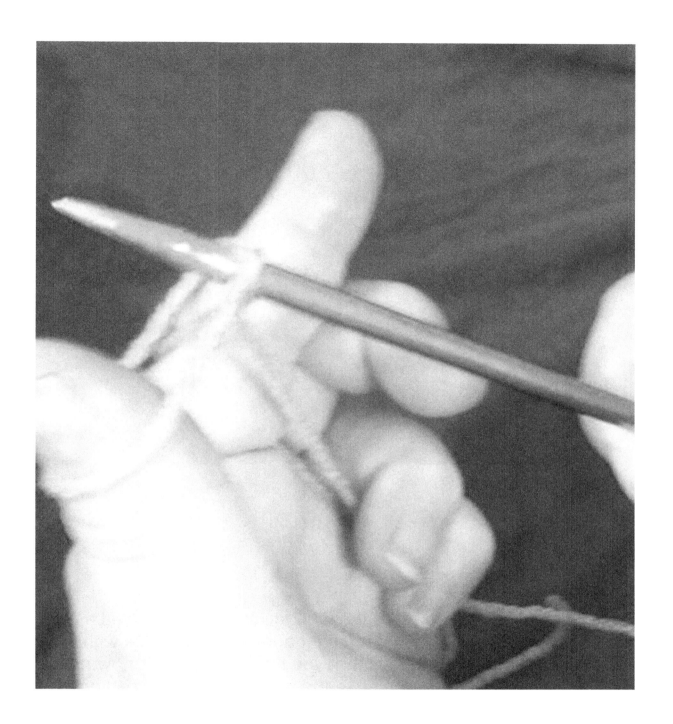

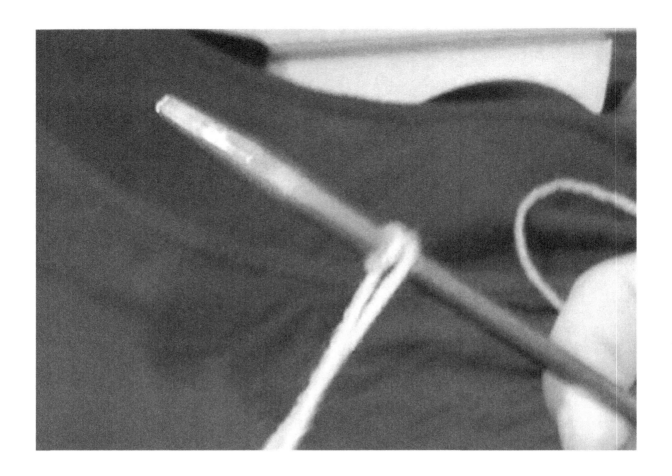

Long Tail Cast On

One of my favorite methods is the long tail cast on. It creates a nice even cast on row which is not too tight and is easy to work with. The disadvantage of this method is that you have to estimate how much yarn you need since you don't use the yarn coming off the skein. An easy way to estimate is to cast on 10 stitches and then mark how much yarn you used. Use this length to estimate how much yarn is needed for the cast on.

To begin hold the yarn like you did for the backward loop, but the yarn from the skein is held over the index finger, and the tail (which is what you'll be casting on) is held over your thumb. With your right hand draw the needle down and up through the loop on your thumb.

Place the needle under the strand of yarn on the index finger and through the loop of the thumb and pull it through. The first cast on will give you two cast on stitches. Repeat the process until you have the correct number of stitches cast on.

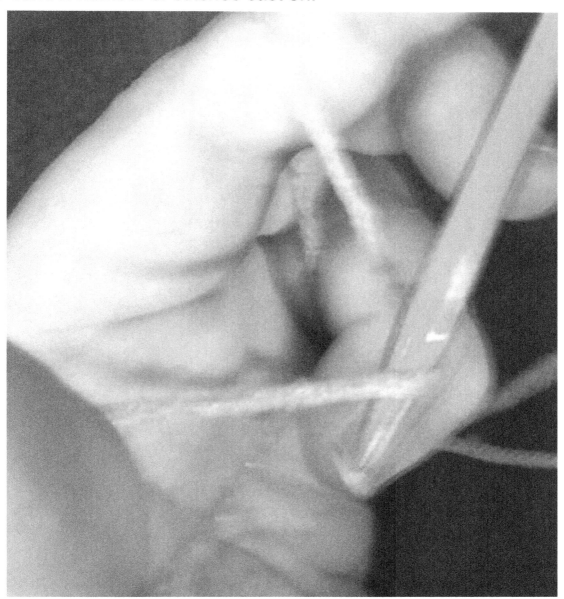

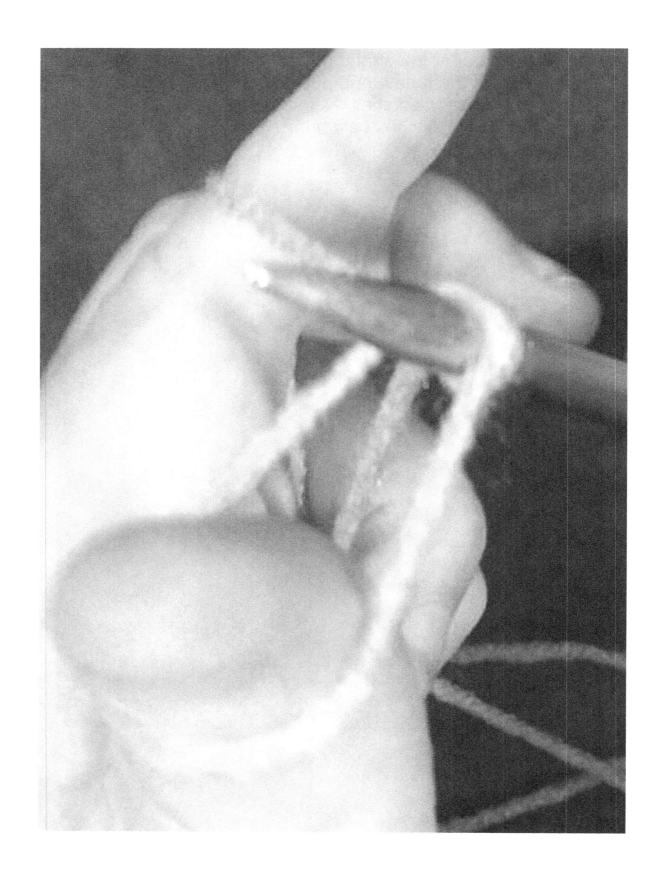

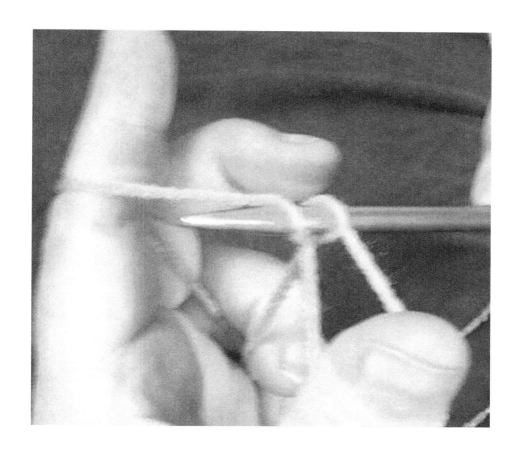

Knit On Cast On Method

Another cast on method I like to use is the knit on method. It produces a nice stretchy cast on row, and knits the first row for you. Begin by placing a slip knot on the left needle. Knit a stitch but don't slip it onto the right needle. Slip it back over onto the left needle instead. Knit the next stitch and slip the loop of that stitch back onto the left needle. Continue to knit stitches and slip them back onto the left needle until you have the correct number of cast on stitches.

Pull the loop of the knit stitch out a bit and then slip it back onto the left needle.

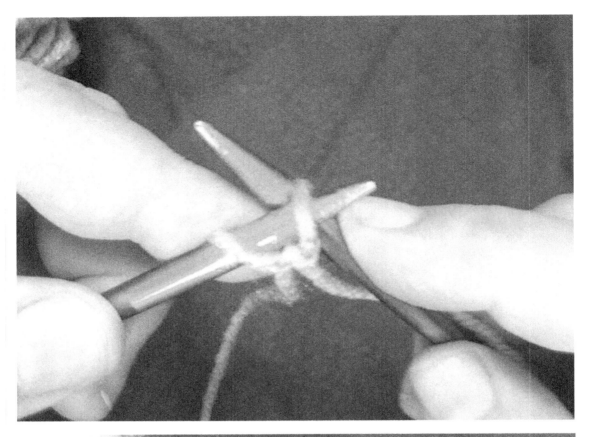

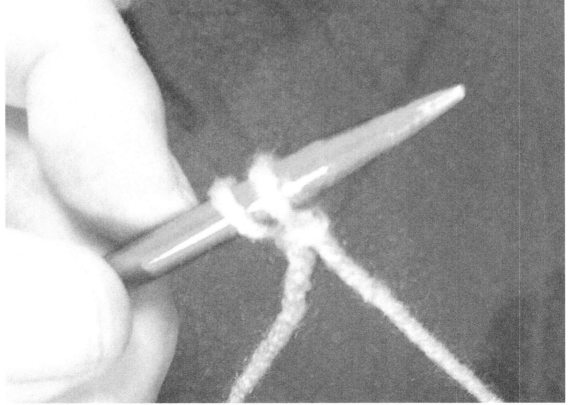

Knit Stitch

I'm right handed so the directions in this book are for right handed knitters. Hold the needle with the cast on stitches in your left hand. Insert the right needle from the front to the back under the first stitch. Wrap the yarn around the needle (known as yarn over) and pull the yarn through the stitch with the tip of the right needle. Slip the new stitch onto the right needle. Holing the yarn in the back of your work slip the tip of the right needle into the next stitch on the left needle from the front to the back, yarn over and draw the yarn through the stitch with the right needle and slip the new stitch onto the right needle. Continue across the row of stitches.

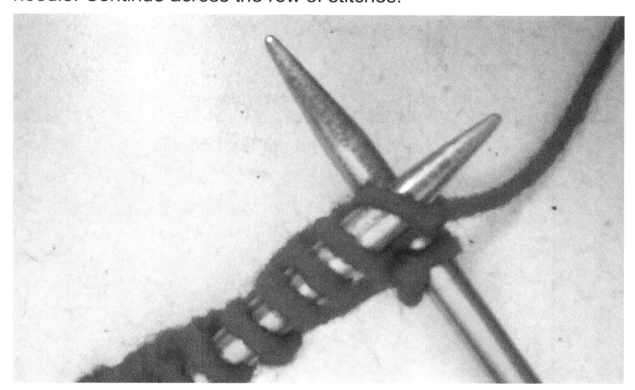

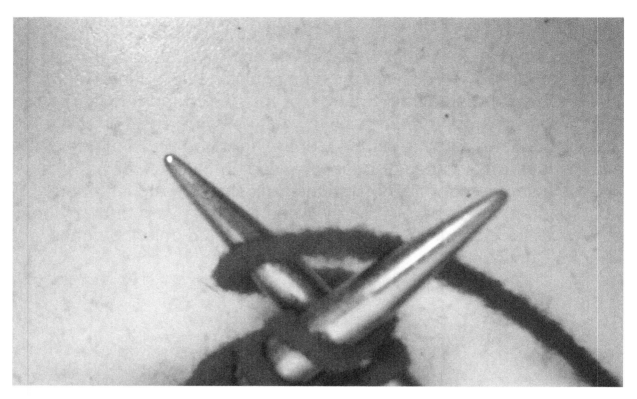

Wrap the yarn around the right needle.

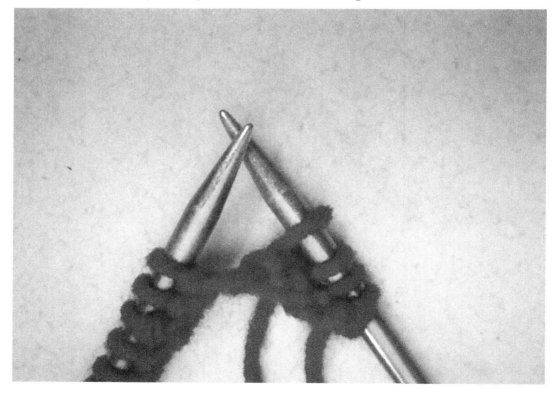

Pull the yarn through the stitch and slip it onto the right needle.

Purl Stitch

Hold the needle with the cast on stitches in your left hand. Insert the tip of the right needle into the first stitch from the back to the front. The tip of the right needle will be in front of the left one. Wrap the yarn around the right needle and draw it through the stitch and slip the new purl stitch onto the right needle. Hold the yarn in the front of your work and insert the needle from the back to the front into the next stitch on the left needle. Yarn

o   ver

and draw the yarn through the stitch and slip the new purl stitch onto the right needle. Continue across the row of stitches.

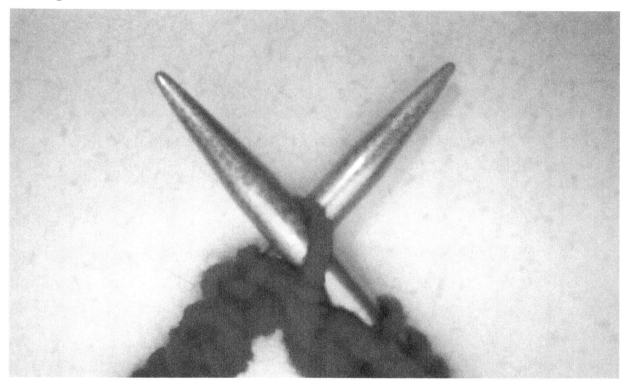

Insert the right needle from the back to the front of the stitch on the left needle.

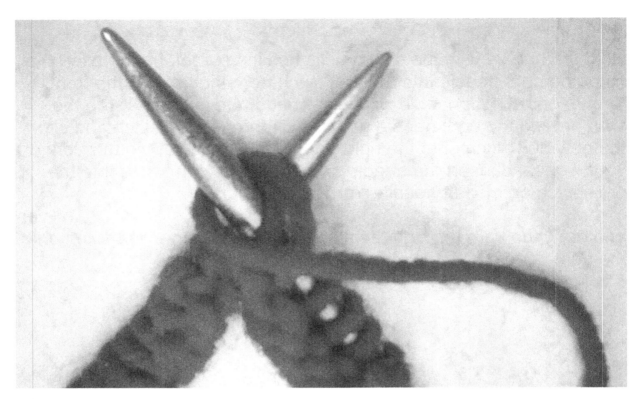

Wrap the yarn around the right needle.

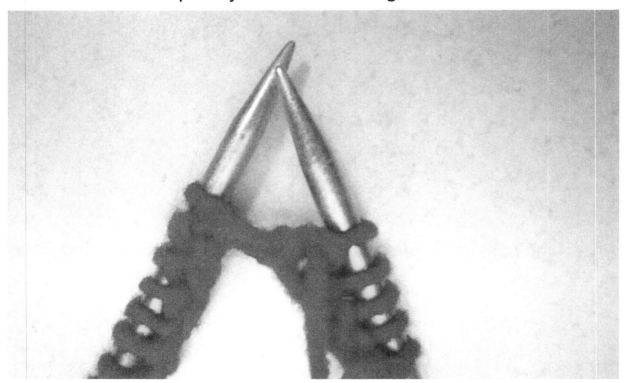

Pull the yarn through the stitch and slip it onto the right needle.

Remember that the yarn is always held in back when you knit, and it is held in the front when you purl. As you switch from knit to purl you will have to pull the yarn to the front. When you switch from purl back to knit, you'll have to pull the yarn to the back. This is important or your stitches won't turn out correctly and you'll be fighting the yarn.

Always count your stitches as you work. This is very important. Knitting is based on stitch counts and building up the pattern from the previous rows. If the stitch count is off in one row the rest of the rows will be off and your pattern won't be correct.

All knit rows are called the garter stitch. Alternating knit and purl rows are called stockinette stitch. You may see these terms in patterns.

Slip Stitches

The slip stitch can be done knitwise, as if to knit, or purlwise, as if to purl. The pattern may tell you to hold the yarn in the front or the back and which way to slip the stitch. If not, then assume it is knitwise with the yarn held in the back. Insert the right needle into the stitch on the left needle as if to purl, and simply slip the stitch onto the right needle. You don't wrap the yarn at all and no stitch is actually knitted. Slip stitches are used in patterns to create lots of different effects.

For example, if you see sl st wyib (slipt stitch with yarn in back) this means you will hold the yarn in the back of your work, insert the needle into the stitch on the left needle as if to purl and slip it onto the right needle.

If you see sl st wyif (slip stitch with yarn in front), pull the yarn to the front and slip the next stitch to the right needle purlwise.

Pay attention to the pattern, it will tell you if you should slip the stitches as if to knit, or to purl. Remember if no instruction is given, then you always slip purlwise.

Binding Off or Casting Off

Once you get your project all knitted up you have to get it off the needles. This is where you bind off, also known as casting off. You can bind of knitwise or purlwise depending on what your pattern calls for. If the pattern doesn't specify bind off knitwise. Knit the first two stitches. Now take the left needle and slip it under the first stitch and pull it over the second one and off the needle. Knit the next stitch and slip the first stitch over it. Continue to do that until you have only one stitch left on the needle. Remove it from the needle, cut the yarn (fasten off) and leave a long tail. Pull the tail through the last stitch and you're done!

Weaving in Tails Securely

When you fasten off the yarn leave at least six inches so you can weave it in securely. Thread a tapestry needle with the tail and weave it in and out of the stitches on the wrong side of the fabric for about an inch. Change direction and weave it in and out for another inch. Change direction once more and weave the tail in and out of the stitches. You may now cut the tail and be assured it won't come undone and start to unravel your project.

Changing Colors

Working with color is fun, and you shouldn't let it intimidate you. When you need to use another color simply pick it up and begin to work with it. Catch the old color under the yarn of the first stitch to secure it and prevent holes in your work. Knit a few stitches and then go back and snug up the yarn to secure the color change.

If you are changing colors at the end of a row and plan on using the color again very soon you can carry it up the side of your work. Let it hang on the side of the fabric and catch it under the yarn of the first stitch of a new row until you need it again up to about four rows. This secures it and you don't have as many tails to weave in.

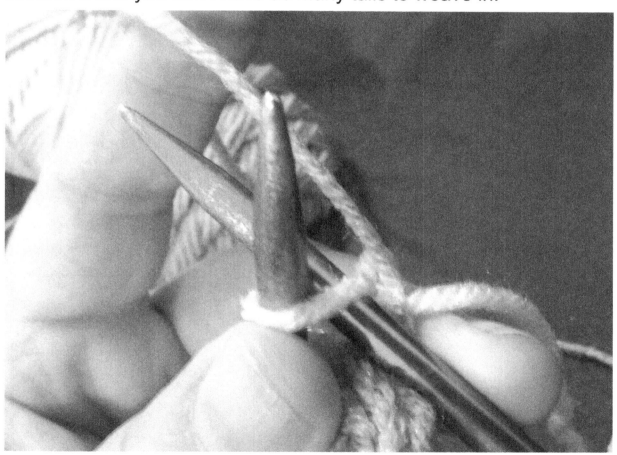

Picking Up a Dropped Stitch

We all drop stitches, it's just a fact of life when you knit. But you don't have to panic if you know how to fix it. You'll need a crochet hook and some patience. When you drop a stitch take the crochet hook and insert it through the loop of the stitch and grab the dropped stitch. Pull the yarn through the loop and place it back on the left needle. For a knit stitch you grab the yarn from the front and for a purl stitch grab the yarn from the back.

Life lines will save your sanity and your project. I use them a lot, even with simple patterns. With a life line if you mess up you don't have to rip out your entire project, you simply rip out rows to the lifeline and then pick up in the pattern and continue on. Thread a tapestry needle with a contrasting piece of yarn long enough to reach across the row. Thread the needle and yarn through the stitches on the needle and remove the tapestry needle. Now leave it. Mark the pattern where you inserted the life line. That way you can tell where you have ripped back to if you need to begin again. As you work move the lifeline up the pattern and make the pattern to keep track.

Designers use a standardized set of abbreviations in patterns. Here is a list of the most commonly used ones today.

Term	Abbreviation
Bind off	BO
Cast on	CO
Decrease	Dec
Increase	Inc
Knit	K
Knit 2 together	K2tog
Knitwise	kwise
Pattern Repeat	*, ( ), [ ]
Place marker	pm

Purl	P
Purl 2 together	P2tog
Purlwise	pwise
Repeat	Rep
Right side	RS
Skip	sk
Slip	sl
Wrong side	WS
Yarn over	Yo

Pattern Repeats

In a pattern you will see asterisks, parenthesis, and brackets with stitch instructions in them. These are pattern repeats. If asterisks are used begin at the first one and knit the stitches to the next one. Then go back to the first one and knit to the next one again. Repeat this as many times as the pattern calls for. For example *k, p3, k* mean you knit 1, purl 3, and knit 1. Then you go back and repeat this sequence as often as the pattern calls for.

Chapter Three – Ribbing

Ribbing us usually used at the cuffs of sleeves, on the bottoms of garments, and anywhere you want to add a bit of texture. Rib stitches are very stretchy so they make the perfect stitches for the openings on garments and at the brim of hats.

When you knit rib stitches you will line up the knit and purl stitches in each row or round. If you are knitting flat (in rows) you will knit and purl across the row, and then in the knit stitches you will purl, and into the purl stitches you will knit across the next row. This creates a ribbed pattern with the knit and purl stitches lined up on both sides of the fabric.

If you are knitting in the round, then you would just repeat the rib pattern around and around since you do not turn your work. The knit and purl stitches line up to create the ribbing pattern.

Knit 1, Purl 1 Ribbing

Cast on an even number of stitches and knit 1, purl 1 across the row. Turn your work. You should have ended with a purl stitch so the first stitch of the new row should be a knit stitch. The knit and purl stiches should line up on both sides of the fabric. If you are knitting in the round, knit 1, purl 1 around each row since you don't turn your work.

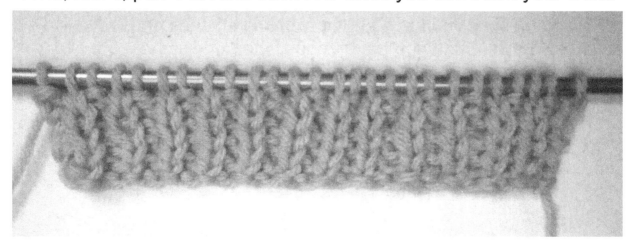

Knit 2, Purl 2 Ribbing

Cast on sets of 4. This means the number of stitches cast on must be divisible by the number 4. Knit 2, purl 2 across the row. Turn your work. Now if you have ended with knit stitches, the first 2 stitches will be purl. If you have ended with purl stitches, the first 2 stitches are knit. This lines up the ribbing pattern in sets of 2.

If you are knitting in the round, just repeat knit 2, purl 2 around the rounds making sure you keep on track and line up the knit and purl stitches.

Notice how the stitches line up to create ribbing.

Knit 2, Purl 3 Ribbing

Begin by casting on sets of 6. Knit 3, purl3 across the row and turn your work. Now if you have ended with knit stitches, the first 3 stitches will be purl. If you have ended with purl stitches, the first 3 stitches are knit. This lines up the ribbing pattern in sets of 3. If you are knitting in the round, just repeat knit 2, purl 2 around the rounds making sure you keep on track and line up the knit and purl stitches.

Staggered Ribbing

You can also create a pretty ribbing pattern by staggering your stitches. In this example I knit 1, purl 1, knit 1 across the row. The actual knitting is k1, p1 *k2, p1* to the last stitch which is a knit stitch. The stitches between the two asterisks are repeated to the last stitch. This an example of a pattern repeat.

Right Side

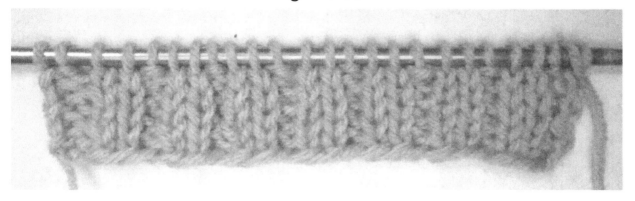

Wrong Side

Experiment with different ribbing patterns. You can have ribbing as small as 1 by 1, or as wide as you like. Just remember if you're working in rows your knit stitches become purl stitches in the next row. This is because when you turn your work you will need to line up the stitches to retain the rib pattern. If you're working in the round then you just continue the ribbing pattern around the rounds.

Chapter Four – Texture with Knit and Purl Stitches

In this chapter we'll explore some fun and creative ways to use simple knit and purl stitches to create texture and patterns in your projects. One of the great things about using knit and purl stitches is most projects are double sided. The right side will have a different texture then the wrong side, but there will be texture and patterns on both sides of the fabric.

Stockinette Stitch

The stockinette stitch is knitted in a two row pattern. The first row is knitted and the second row is purled. The right side of the fabric is smooth with V's of stitches lined up in rows. The wrong side of the fabric is bumpy and has what are known as purl bumps. When knitting in rows you will knit one row and purl the next. If you are knitting in the round then you would only have to knit each row since you don't turn your work.

Right Side

Wrong Side
Garter Stitch

The garter stitch is very easy. You knit each row. This creates a lovely texture and the garter stitch does not roll up like the stockinette stitch. If you are knitting in the round, then you would need to purl each row to achieve the same look. The right and wrong side look exactly alike since you are knitting all rows.

By combing stockinette and garter stitches you can create patterns and texture in you knit projects. You can also use garter and stockinette stitches to create a frame for your projects.

In this example you can see how rows of garter stitches form the top and bottom "frame" for this dishcloth. The knit stitches on the sides keep the dishcloth from rolling up and also create a frame for the basket weave stitches.

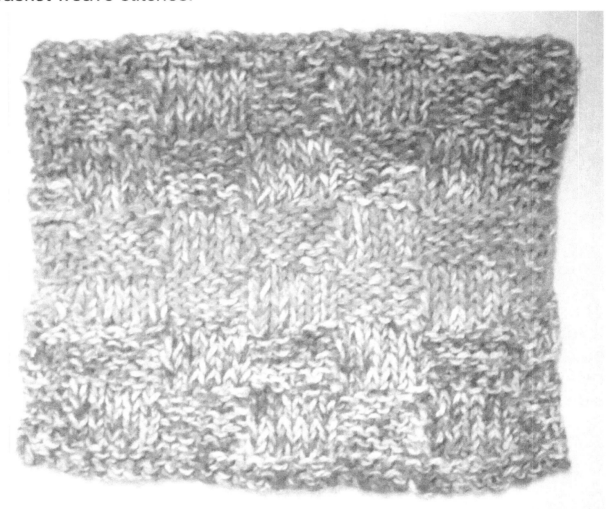

You can also see how combining knit and purl stitches and alternating them creates a basket weave effect. (I'll include the pattern for this dishcloth at the end of this book.)

By alternating stockinette and garter rows you can also frame a feature of a pattern. In this bag pattern the eyelet stitches are framed by rows of garter stitches which make them pop. Without the garter rows, the eyelet pattern wouldn't be as striking.

Using Knit and Purl Stitches to Create Patterns

In the basket weave dishcloth, you can see how using knit and purl stitches create a pretty pattern. You can also use knit and purl stitches to create patterns and pictures in your knitting.

In the following examples you can see how using knit and purl stitches create a pretty heart design. You can use this technique to create any type of pattern or picture you want in your projects. Also notice the garter rows and knit stitches which form a frame and keep the square from rolling up on itself.

Seed Stitch

The seed stitch creates a bumpy fabric which is great for dishcloths and washcloths. It is also a nice addition of texture to a project. Unlike ribbing you will be working knit stitches into knit stitches and purl stitches into the purl stitches on the next row. This staggers the purl bumps and creates a pretty texture.

Cast on an even number of stitches. Knit 1, purl 1 across the row. Turn your work. Purl 1, knit 1 across the next row. Alternate the rows until you have the desired length.

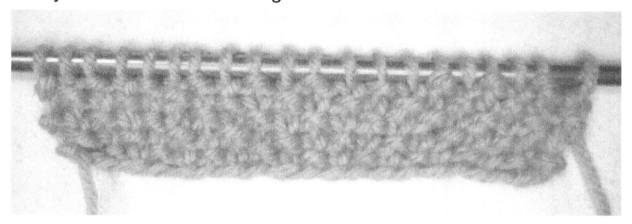

Eyelet Stitch

The eyelet stitch is a combination of knit and yarn overs. A yarn over is exactly what it sounds like, you place the yarn over the needle before you knit two stitches together.

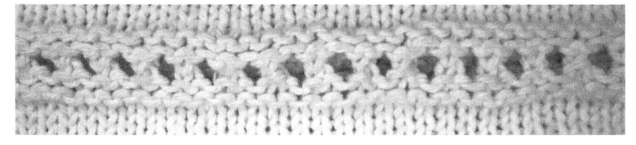

First place the yarn over the right needle.

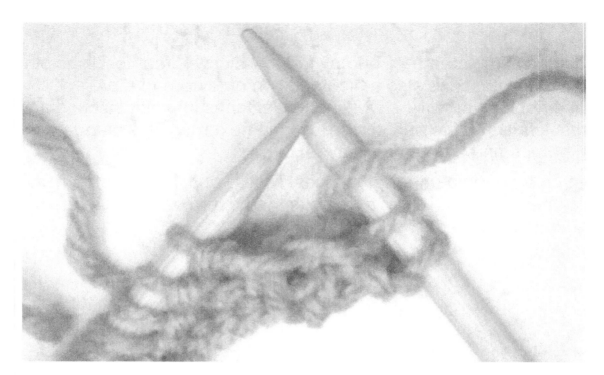

Next insert the right needle under two stitches on the left needle as if to nit. Knit both stitches together. Now when you knit or purl back across the row the yarn over will create a pretty eyelet in the fabric.

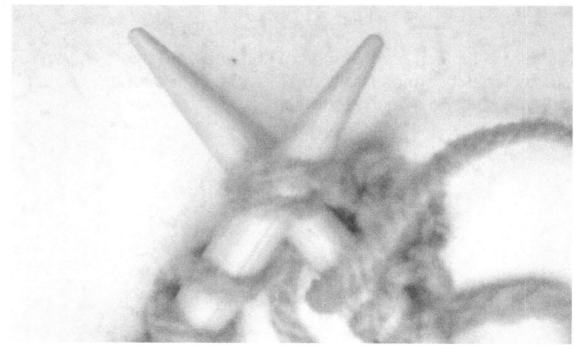

Drop Stitch

The drop stitch is a fun way to add a lot of texture and interest to your projects. It also uses yarn overs and knit stitches. First yarn over once or twice depending on the look you want. Knit the next stitch. Continue to yarn over and knit across the row. It works best if you knit the first two and the last two stitches of the drop stitch row.

When you come back across the row, knit or purl the knit stitches and let the yarn overs fall of the needle. It may seem strange to drop stitches on purpose, but this is what creates the pattern.

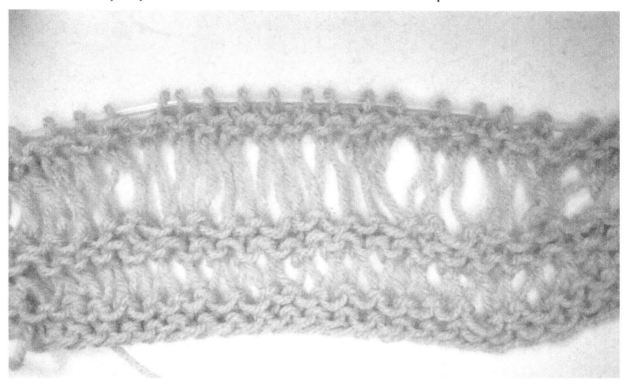

The first set of drop stitches is a single yarn over. The top set of drop stitches were created with two yarn overs. You can see how the double yarn over creates a much looser texture.

Chapter Five – Fun Beginner Patterns

Now that we've learned the basics of knitting and how you can use knit and purl stitches to create texture in knitting, let's practice with some simply beginner patterns. Refer to the abbreviation table in Chapter Two for the patterns in this chapter.

Basket Weave Dishcloth

You will need a skein each of cotton yarn in two colors. I used Premier Home yarn in Violet Splash (Color A) and Sahara Splash (Color B)

The pattern is knitted in sets of 5 plus 6. So you can make the washcloth larger or smaller as long as you cast on sets of 5 and then 6 more for the edging stitches.

With Color A CO 31

Rows 1-3: k

Row 4: k3 *p5, k5* rep ending with p5, k3

Row 5: k3 *k5, p5* rep ending with k5, k3

Row 6: Repeat Row 4

Row 7: Repeat Row 5

Row 8: Repeat Row 4

Row 9: k3 * p5, k5* rep ending with p5, k3

Row 10: k3 *k5, p5* rep ending with k5, k3

Row 11: Repeat Row 9

Row 12: Repeat Row 10

Row 13: Repeat Row 9

With Color B

Rows 14-23: Repeat Rows 4-13

With Color A

Rows 24-32: Repeat Rows 4-13

Rows 33-35: k, BO and weave in tails.

Drop Stitch Scarf

Cowl measures about 9 inches wide and around 58-60 inches long.

You will need size 15 (10mm) knitting needles and 1 skein of Premier Home yarn in Grape Splash. You will also need a tapestry needle. (You can use any yarn you have on hand. If you use a thicker yarn the cowl will be shorter, but still very pretty.)

Gauge is not important for this project.

Cast on 30

Row 1 & 2: k

Row 3: k1 *yo twice, k1* rep to last st, k1

Row 3-5: k

Row: 6: k1, *yo, k1* rep to last st, k1

Rows 12-16: k

Rows 13-30: Repeat Rows 6-12 twice

Row 31: k1 *yo twice, k1* rep to last st, k1

Rows 32-38: k

Row 39: k1, *yo, k1* rep to last st, k1

Rows 40-45: k

Rows 46-57: Repeat Rows 39-45 twice

Row 58: k1 *yo twice, k1* rep to last st, k1

Rows 59-64: k

Row 65: k1, *yo, k1* rep to last st, k1

Rows 66-70: k

Rows 71-82: Repeat Rows 65-70 twice

Row 83: *yo twice, k1* rep to last st, k1

Rows 84-89: k

Row 90: k1, *yo, k1* rep to last st, k1

Rows 91-96: k

Rows 97-103: Repeat Rows 90-96

0Row 104: k1, *yo, k1* rep to last st, k1

Rows 105-107: k, cast off knitwise after Row 107, weave in tails and block lightly with your hands.

Add fringe on the ends if you'd like. You could also sew the end together to make a cute infinity scarf.

Seed Stitch Square

I knitted this up to be part of a larger project and used Red Heart Super Saver in Hot Pink, but you can use cotton yarn and make this pattern into a dishcloth or wash cloth.

CO 30

Rows 1-3: k

Row 4: k4 *k1, p1* k4

Row 5-34: Repeat Row 4

Rows 35-37: k

BO and weave in tails

Eyelet Cowl

I really like to knit up cowls. They work up quickly and make great gifts. I used knit, purl, yarn over and knit 2 together stitches to create a highly textured pattern which looks much more complicated than it really is.

You will need a skein of acrylic or any medium weight yarn. I used Red Heart Super Saver in Shocking Pink. You will also need a 24 inch size 8 circular needle and a tapestry needle.

Cast on 150

Rnds 1 & 2: k

Rnd 3: p

Rnd 4: k

Rnd 5: p

Rnd 6: *yo, k2tog, k1* rep around

Rnd 7: *k1, yo, k2tog* rep around

Rnds 8-14: k

Rnd 15-19: Rep Rnds 3-7

Rnd 20: p

Rnd 21: k

Rnd 22: p

Rnds 23 & 24: k

BO and weave in tails.

Thank you for purchasing this book on using knit and purl stitches to create texture in your knitting projects. Feel free to sell anything you make from the patterns in this book, but please share the link to the book if you want to share a pattern.

I hope you enjoy learning how to knit and experimenting with texture in your projects. Until next time take care!

GRANNY SQUARE BASICS

Learn How to Crochet and Join Granny Square Motifs

By Violet Henderson

Contents

Chapter One – Stitches Used in This Book

Before we begin to learn how to crochet Granny Squares I thought it would be a good idea to include a chapter on the basic crochet stitches and techniques used to create Granny Square motifs and projects. If you're a beginner, this chapter will serve as a quick tutorial on basic stitches and techniques while if you're a bit more advanced you can use this chapter as a reference and refresher. No matter what your skill level, Granny Squares are easy to master. So, let's get started!

Abbreviations

Designers use a standardized set of abbreviations for stitches and instructions. Each pattern should have a key for the abbreviations used in the pattern. Be sure to check it just in case the designer has included unique ones in their pattern. Here are the most common abbreviations used in patterns written in US terms.

Stitch Name	Abbreviation
Chain stitch	Ch
Stitch/Stitches	St/sts
Slip stitch	Sl st
Single crochet	Sc
Double crochet	Dc
Half double crochet	Hdc
Treble crochet	Trb
Repeat	Rep
Single crochet 2 together	Sc2tog
Double crochet 2 together	Dc2tog
Half double crochet 2 together	Hdc2tog

You may also find patterns written in UK terms. Use this table to help translate the abbreviations into US terms.

US Terms		UK Terms	
Chain	Ch	Chain	Ch
Slip stitch	Sl st	Slip stitch	Ss
Single crochet	Sc	Double crochet	Dc
Half double crochet	Hdc	Half treble	Htr
Double crochet	Dc	Treble	Tr
Treble crochet	Trb	Double treble	dtr

Basic Crochet Stitches and Techniques

While you are first learning to crochet, concentrate on handling the hook and yarn. Get used to using them and focus on technique. Take your time and don't worry if you have to rip out (also known as frog) your stitches. We all have to do that sometimes, no matter how proficient we are at crochet. Relax and have fun, remember crochet is supposed to be enjoyable.

Chain Stitch

The chain stitch is used for foundation chains and to create spaces in patterns. First create a slip knot and place it on the hook. Place the yarn over the hook (known as a yarn over) and pull the yarn through the slip knot on the hook. This if the first chain stitch. Yarn over and pull the yarn through the loop on the hook. This is the second chain stitch. Continue this until you have the appropriate number of chain stitches. Concentrate on getting your stitches even and getting used to handling the hook and yarn. Speed will come later, right now concentrate on technique.

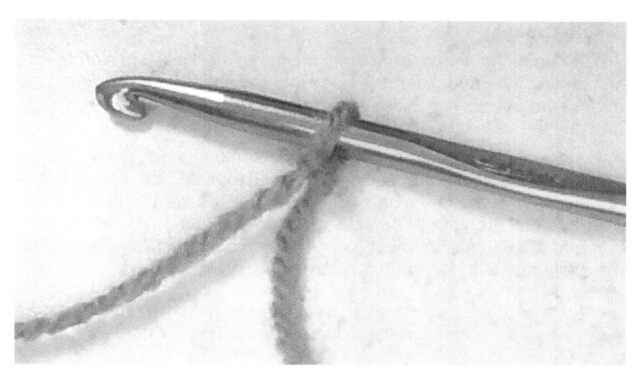

Slip knot

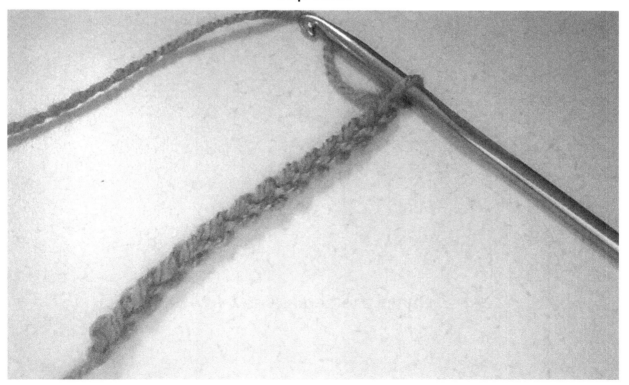

Chain stitch

Single Crochet

When beginning with a foundation chain, you will need to skip the first chain stitch and insert the hook into the second chain from the hook. Yarn over and pull the yarn through the chain stitch. Yarn over and pull the yarn other the two loops on the hook.

If you are beginning a row or round with single crochet, chain one and count this as the first stitch. Insert the hook into the next stitch, not the base of the chain one, yarn over, pull the yarn through, yarn over and pull the yarn through the two loops on the hook. When you come to the end of the row the last single crochet is then worked into the chain one stitch at the beginning of the previous row.

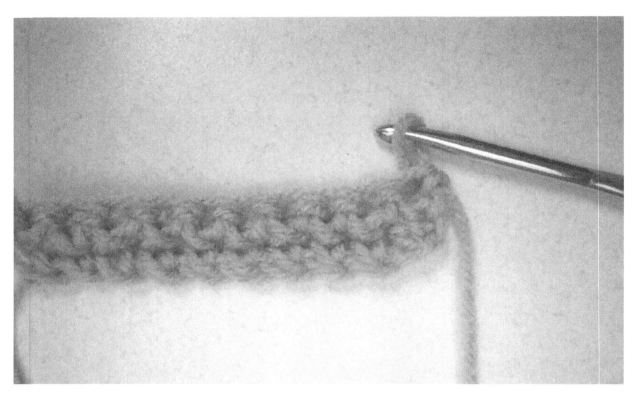

Chain 1 to begin a new row

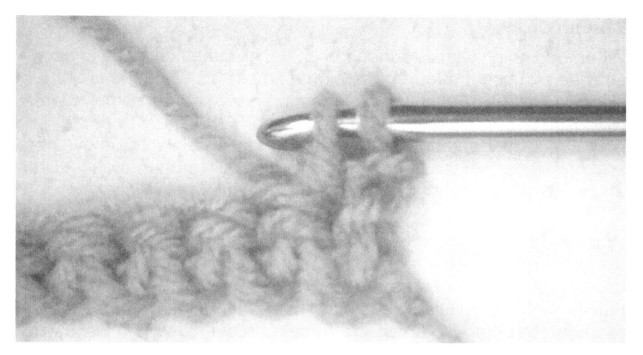

Work the first stitch into the next stitch, not the base of the chain 1.

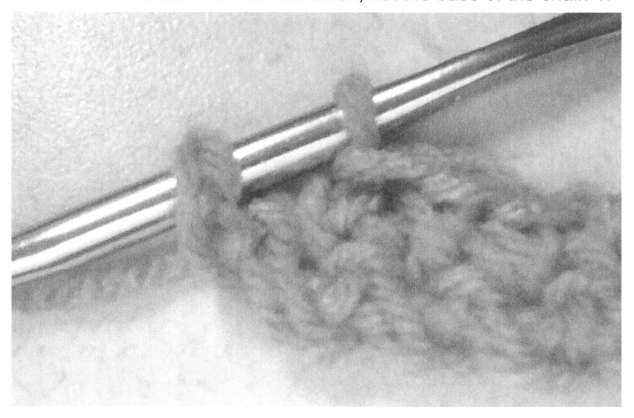

The last stitch is worked into the chain 1 of the previous row.

Double Crochet

When beginning with a foundation chain, skip the first three chain stitches and use the fourth one for the first stitch. The first three skipped chains are counted as the first double crochet stitch in the row. Yarn over and insert the hook into the fourth chain from the hook. Yarn over and pull the yarn through the chain stitch. Now there are three loops on the hook. Yarn over and pull through the first two loops, yarn over and pull through the last two loops to finish the stitch.

When beginning a new row, chain three. This counts as the first stitch. Yarn over and insert the hook into the next stitch, not into the base of the chain three, yarn over and pull through, yarn over and pull through the first two loops, yarn over and pull through the last two loops to complete the stitch. At the end of the row the last stitch is worked into the third starting chain of the previous row (also known as the turning chain),

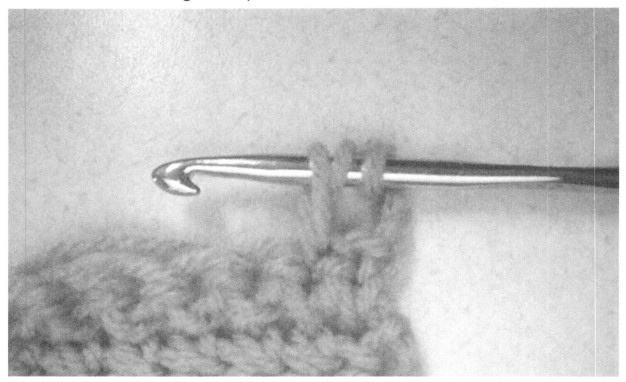

Yarn over and insert the hook into the next stitch, yarn over and pull through.

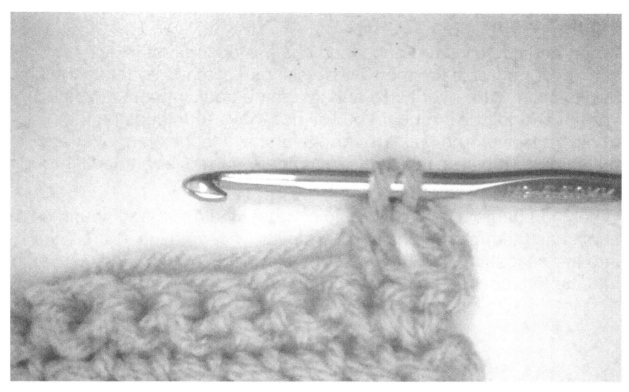

Yarn over and pull through the first two loops on the hook.

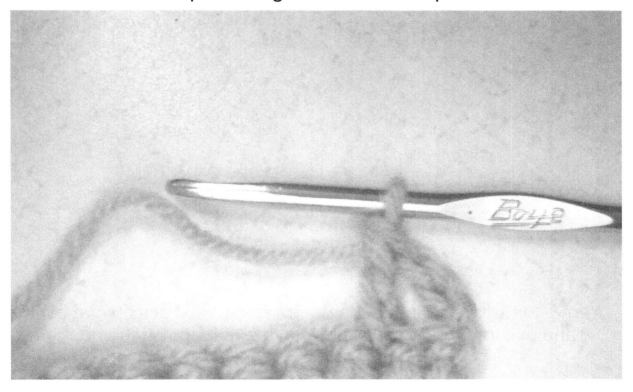

Yarn over and pull through the last two loops to complete the stitch.

Treble Crochet

When beginning with a foundation chain, skip the first five chain stitches for a treble crochet. These skipped stitches count as the first treble stitch. Yarn over twice and insert the hook into the next stitch, yarn over and pull through. You will now have four loops on the hook. Yarn over and pull through the first two loops, yarn over and pull through the next two loops, and finally yarn over and pull through the last two loops to complete the stitch.

When you begin a row with treble crochet, chain five and count these chains as the first treble stitch. Yarn over twice and insert the hook into the next stitch, not the base of the chain five. Work the last stitch into the fifth chain of the turning chain of the previous row.

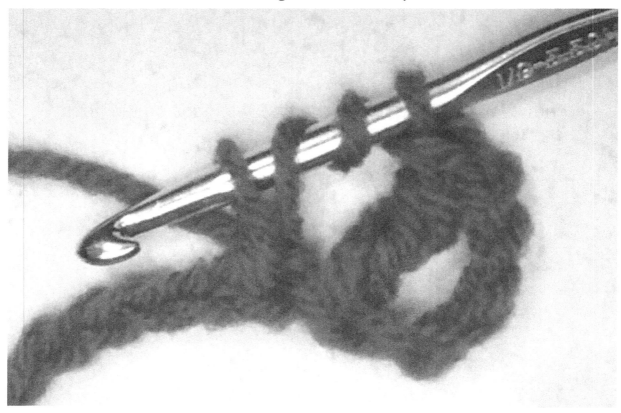

Yarn over twice and insert the hook into the next stitch, yarn over and pull through. You will now have four loops on the hook.

Yarn over and pull through two loops on the hook three times to complete the stitch.

Slip Stitch

A slip stitch is used to join rounds with crocheting in the round, and to move the yarn into the proper place for the next stitch. Insert the hook into the stitch, yarn over and pull the yarn through the stitch and the hook. No stitch is crocheted, but the yarn is moved, or the round is closed.

Front and Back Post Stitches

Each crochet stitch has a post and top loops which form a V shape. Front and back post stitches are worked around the post as opposed to into the top loops of the stitch. These types of stitches are used to create horizontal and vertical ridges in crochet depending on which side of the fabric they are worked. They can also be used to create attractive cables.

On the right side front post stitches create vertical ridges, and on the wrong side they create horizontal ridges. Back post stitches create horizontal ridges on the right side and vertical ridges on the wrong side.

For example, to begin a front post double crochet yarn over and insert the needle from the front to the back around the post of the stitch in the previous row. Yarn over and pull the yarn up even with the stitches in the active row. Yarn over and pull through two loops, yarn over and pull through the last two loops.

The hook goes around the post from front to back.

To crochet a back post double crochet, yarn over and insert the hook from the back to the front around the post. Yarn over and pull the yarn up even with the active stitches, yarn over and pull through two loops, and yarn over and pull through the last two loops to complete the stitch.

The hook goes around the post from back to front. It helps to pinch the fabric a bit to make it easier to insert the hook.

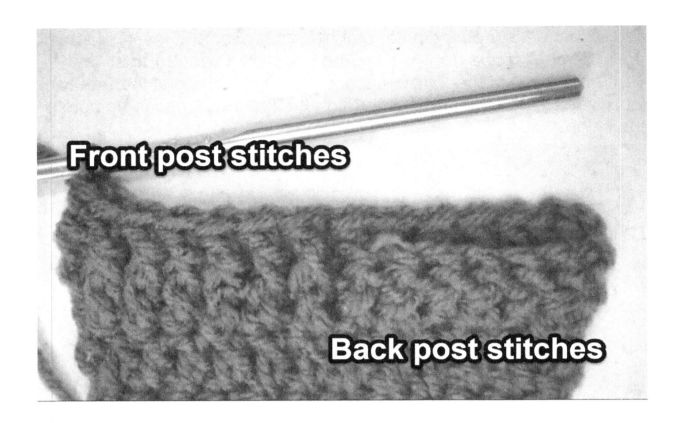

Front post stitches

Back post stitches

Decreases

A decrease is done by crocheting more than one stitch together. For example, if you see the abbreviation dc2tog this mean you will double crochet two stitches as one. Yarn over and insert the hook into the next stitch, yarn over and pull through. Yarn over and pull through the first two loops on the hook. You will have two loops on the hook.

Yarn over and insert the hook into the next stitch, yarn over and pull through. Yarn over and pull through the first two loops on the hook. You now have three loops on the hook. Yarn over and pull the yarn through all three loops at once. This crochets two stitches as one and decreases the number of stitches in a row or round by one.

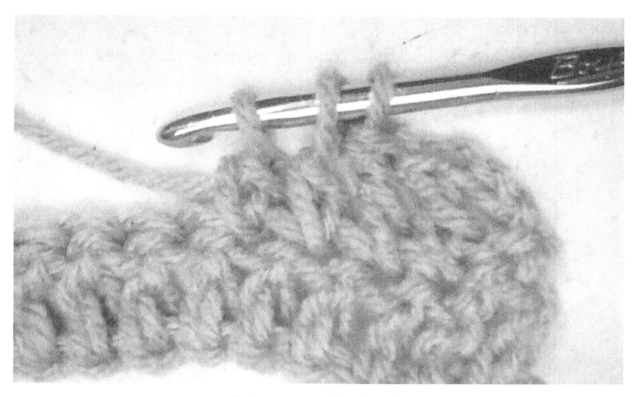

3 loops on the hook

Completed decrease (dc2tog)

Shell Stitches

Shell stitches are created by crocheting more than one stitch into a single stitch. In this example you can see there are three double crochet all worked into one stitch forming a shell.

Attaching or Joining a New Color

When you add a new color to a Granny Square it is best to attach, or join, the new color with a slip knot. Create a slip knot and place it on your hook. Insert the hook into the proper stitch, yarn over and draw the yarn through the stitch and the loop on the hook. This securely joins the new color to the crochet fabric.

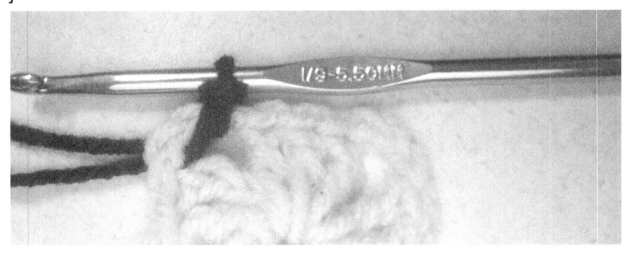

Weaving in Tails

Weaving in the tails of yarn securely is a very important step. This ensures your work doesn't unravel and the stitches don't work themselves loose. When you fasten off yarn always leave at least six inches. This gives you plenty to work with when weaving in the tails.

Thread a blunt end or tapestry needle with the tail, and on the wrong side of the fabric weave the tail in and out of the stitches for about an inch. Turn the fabric and weave the tail in and out of the stitches on the wrong side again for about an inch. Now turn the fabric one last time and weave the tail in and out of the stitches for another inch.

Always turn the fabric at least three times and weave the tails carefully into the stitches on the wrong side of the fabric to secure them. Now you can trim the tail and know that your yarn is secure.

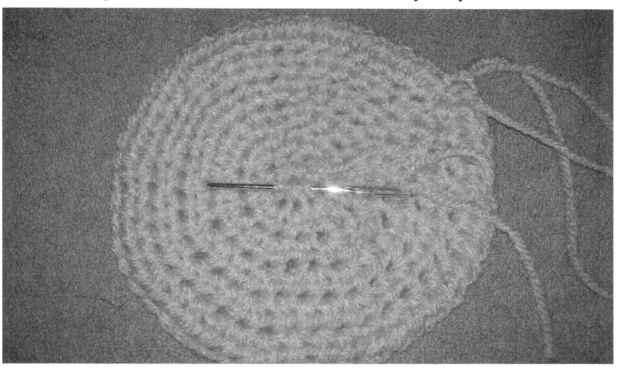

First one way for about an inch

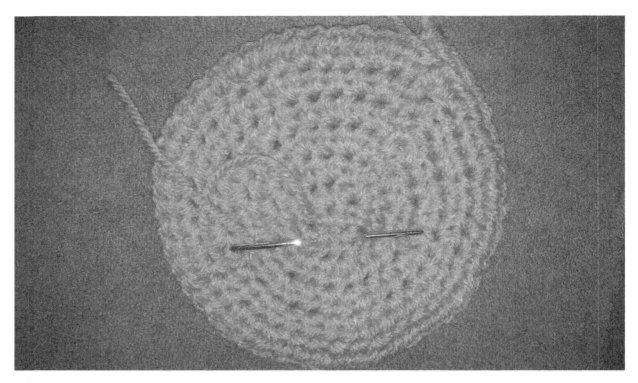

Turn the fabric and weave in for another inch

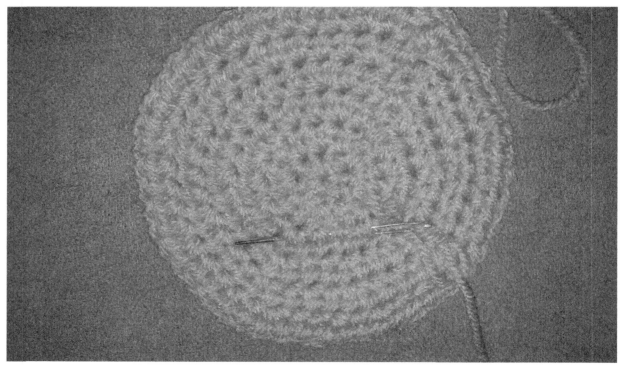

Turn it one last time and weave in the tail for another inch, now you can cut your yarn and the tail will be secure.

Chapter Two – How to Crochet a Granny Square

Granny Squares are crocheted in the round. This means you don't crochet back and forth in rows, but around and around in a counterclockwise direction. Each round is completed with a slip stitch into the top of the starting chain of the round.

Granny Squares have a natural lean to them because of the tension of the stitches. As you go around the square the stitches naturally pull and create a "wonky" center. If you want a perfectly square motif, turn your work after each round and this will prevent the center of the Granny Square from becoming crooked. It is up to you if you want to turn the square, or just continue around and around.

Construction of a Granny Square

Granny Squares consist of groups of 3 double crochet shells separated by either a chain 1 or chain 3. In each corner you will work 2 double crochet shells separated by 3 chain stitches. Along the sides the shells are separated by a 1 chain stitch. As you work there will always be four corners of 3 double crochet, chain 3, 3 double crochet, chain 1. As the square grows there will be more 3 double crochet shells separate by 1 chain stitch.

This will become clearer when we actually begin to crochet a Granny Square.

Round 1

To begin chain four and join with a slip stitch into the first chain stitch to form a ring. The stitches of the first round are worked into the center of the ring, not into the chain stitches.

Chain 3, this counts as the first double crochet, work 2 more double crochet and chain 3. Work 3 double crochet and chain 3. Repeat 3 double crochet, chain 3 twice more. Join with a slip stitch into the 3rd chain of the starting chain (the beginning chain 3). This is Round 1. You will have four sets of shells separated by chain 3 spaces.

Round 1

Now you can either begin a new color, or use the same one for the next round. If you choose to continue on with the same color, you will need to move the yarn to the chain 3 corner space. Slip stitch into the 2 double crochet stitches along the side and into the chain 3 space. This will put your yarn in the proper position to begin the next row. Chain 3 to begin Round 2.

If you choose to begin a new color, pull up a long tail and fasten off (cut) the yarn. Pull the tail to the wrong side to secure it, and either weave it in now or when you complete the square.

Place a slip knot on the hook and insert the hook into any chain 3 space. Draw the yarn through the slip knot securing the yarn onto the chain three space. Now you're ready to begin the next round. Use this technique each time you change colors on a new round. Always join the new color in a chain 3 corner space.

Chain 3 (counts as the first double crochet in the shell) and work 2 double crochet into the chain 3 corner space. Chain 3, 3 double crochet into the same chain 3 space. Chain 1. Into each chain 3 space crochet 3double crochet, chain 3, 3 double crochet, chain 1. Join into the 3rd beginning chain, draw up a long tail and fasten off.

Round 2

If you look at this round you will see each corner section is separated by a chain 1 space. This chain 1 space is where the side shells are worked. As the Granny Square grows you will always have 4 corner chain 3 sections, but the number of chain 1 spaces on the sides will increase.

Round 3

Join a new color in any chain 3 space. Chain3 and work 2 double crochet, chain 3, 3 double crochet, chain 1 into this chain 3 space. Into the next chain 1 space work 3 double crochet and chain 1. Into each corner chain 3 space work 3 double crochet, chain 3, 3 double crochet, chain 1. Into each chain 1 space work 3 double crochet, chain 1. Work around the Granny Square and join with a slip stitch into the 3rd chain of the beginning chain.

You can add as many rounds as you like to your square, and change colors as often or as little as you like. Remember to work 3 double crochet, chain 3, 3 double crochet, chain 1 into each chain 3 corner space, and 3 double crochet, chain 1 into each side chain 1 space. The beginning chain 3 always counts as the first double crochet in the first shell. And you join into the 3rd chain of this beginning chain to complete each round.

Here is an example of a large Granny Square throw. You can see how the middle is crooked because of the way the tension of the rounds. You can fix this by turning the square after each round when you join a color or continue with the same color.

Here is another example of a Granny Square afghan. The artist used Granny Squares and Granny rounds along with varying sizes of squares to create this stunning work of art.

There are lots of possibilities once you learn how to crochet Granny Squares. They're not just for afghans and throws. You can create pretty bags, hats, garments, and home accessories using Granny Squares and your imagination.

On the following page you will see a cute box hat and cowl made with Granny Squares and Granny rows. This set reminds me of a sock monkey and would be cute for all ages.

Chapter Three – Solid Granny Square

Sometimes you may want a more solid look to your project. This is where a solid Granny Square comes in handy. Instead of using chain stitches to separate the shells, you will work double crochet stitches along the sides and use a chain 1 space to create the corner.

Round 1

Begin by chaining 4 and joining with a slip stitch into the first chain to create a ring. Chain 3 (counts as the first double crochet) work 4 double crochet into the ring, chain 1. Work 5 double crochet into the ring and chain 1. Repeat 5 double crochet, chain 1 twice more and join into the 3rd beginning chain, and fasten off if you wish to change colors.

Round 2

If you have fastened off the first color, join the next color in a corner chain 1 space and chain 3, or begin the round with a chain 3. Work a double crochet into each stitch across the side. Into the next chain 1 space work double crochet, chain 1, double crochet. Continue to work a double crochet into each stitch and double crochet, chain 1, double crochet into each chain 1 space around. Join into the 3rd beginning chain. You should have 7 double crochet across each side separated by a chain 1 for the corner.

Round 3

As your square increases in size, the number of double crochet stitches along with sides will increase by 2 for each round. In Round 3 you will have 9 double crochet across the sides and a chain 1 space in each corner. In the next round you will have 11, 13, 15, and so on until you reach the desired size of your square.

To begin Round 3 chain 3 or join a new color in a chain 1 space. (If you continue with the same color you will have to crochet the last corner and then crochet to the beginning chain to join because the beginning chain 3 will be in a side stitch, not in the corner.)

Chapter Four – Joining Methods

There are lots of ways to join your Granny Squares once you have them all crocheted up. In this chapter we'll go over a few of the most popular and easy methods to join your squares.

Whip Stitch Join

The whip stitch join creates an almost braided look between the squares. To begin hold two squares with the right sides together. Match up the stitches on the sides and with a tapestry needle threaded with yarn insert the needle into the 2nd chain stitch of a corner space. Insert the needle into the squares of both stitches and work your way across the squares catching only the outside loops of the side stitches in the seam. When you reach the next corner, pick up two more squares, hold them wrong sides together, and continue to whip stitch across the sides.

Begin in the 2nd chain stitch of a corner space and work your way across the sides using the outer loops of the stitches.

I used a contrasting color so you could see the seam.

The same seam using a matching color.

Single Crochet Join

The single crochet join forms a pretty border around the squares. Begin by holding two squares with the wrong sides together. Join the yarn into the chain 3 corner space and chain 1. Single crochet into the chain 3 space and into both stitches of the squares across. Single crochet into each chain 1 space across the side. When you reach the end of the square, pick up two more squares holding them wrong sides together. Single crochet into the chain 3 space of the first squares, chain 1, single crochet into the chain 3 space of the next two squares.

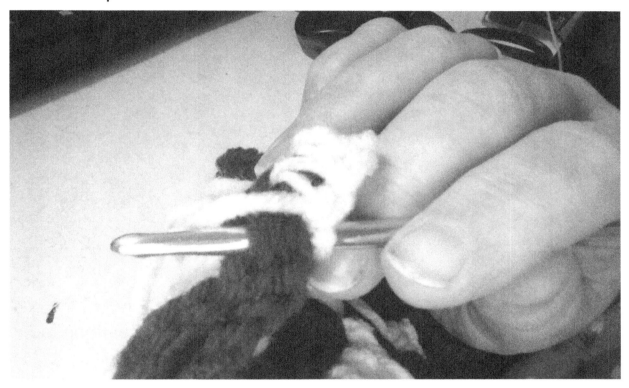

Be sure to catch both loops of the stitches on both squares into the single crochet stitches.

Once you have a row of squares joined and you want to join another row, you will need to hold the rows with the wrong sides facing. Join the yarn at the end chain 3 space and chain 1. Single crochet into the chain 3 space and into each stitch to the corner. Where four squares meet single crochet into the chain 3 space, slip stitch around the chain 1 and single crochet into the next chain 3 space. This creates a nice tight even join in the corners.

Notice the pretty ridge formed by the single crochet seam on the right side.

I find it easier to join rows of squares together, and then join these rows. That way you have nice long seams to work with and I think it makes your project look more professional and finished.

Whip Stitch Join

The whip stitch join is similar to the single crochet join, but it does not create a raised ridge. Hold two squares with the right sides together and join the yarn in any chain 3 space. Chain 1 and the slip stitch across the sides of the squares. You can either use both loops of the stitches, or just the outside loops. Continue across the squares and at the next corner slip stich into the chain 3 space, chain 1, and slip stitch into the next chain 3 space of the next two squares.

Right side of slip stitch join

When you are joining rows of squares crochet, join the corners by slip stitching into the corner, slip stitch around the chain 1, and slip stitch into the next corner. This creates a nice tight and even join for the corners. I prefer to use a matching color for a slip stitch join since it blends in better than a contrasting color.

Join As You Go Method

The join as you go method is a fun challenge. What you do is use the last round of the squares to join them together. Work the first square completely. Work the next square and on the last round work two sides and at the third corner chain 1. Pick up the first square and hold the squares with the wrong sides together. Slip stitch into both chain 3 spaces of the squares. Chain 1. Work 3 double crochet into the second square's chain 3 space.

Instead of chaining 1, you will now slip stitch into the chain 1 space of the first square. Work 3 double crochet into the second square's chain 3 space, chain 1, slip stitch into both square's chain 3 spaces, chain 1, and finish the corner of the second square with 3 double crochet. You may now complete the last side of the second square as usual.

First two squares joined

Work the next square and on the last round work the first corner and across one side. At the next corner chain 1, pick up the squares that have been joined and slip stitch into the corner space. Chain 1 and work 3 double crochet into the corner space of the square you are crocheting. Slip stitch into the chain 1 space of the square you are joining to and 3 double crochet into the chain 1 space of the square you are crocheting. At the corner where the three squares meet, chain 1, slip stitch into the slip stitches, chain 1, and work 3 double crochet into the corner of the square you are working on. Continue with the last round around the square and fasten off.

3 squares joined

As you continue to join squares you will be able to see which sides you will need to complete and which side you will join as you complete them. On the sides you are joining, slip stitch into the 2nd chain stitch of each corner, and into each chain 1 space.

4 squares joined

There are other ways to join Granny Squares that I don't cover in this chapter. If you look on YouTube you will find videos on the braided join, flat braided join, and other types of joins. Each one gives you a different type of look and feel to your projects.

Final Step

Before you begin any type of edging is it always a good idea to do one round of single crochet completely around your project. Work single crochet stitches into each stitch around, working 3 single crochet into the corners. This round of single crochet stitches gives you a nice even base to work the edging stitches.

Then you can work any type of edging you like. Personally I like a scalloped or shell edging.

To crochet a scalloped edging work the following sequence around the afghan or throw: single crochet, double crochet, treble crochet, double crochet, single crochet.

For a shell edging single crochet and skip one stitch, work 3 double crochet into the next stitch, skip one stitch and repeat the pattern around the afghan or throw.

Thank You!

Printed in Great Britain
by Amazon